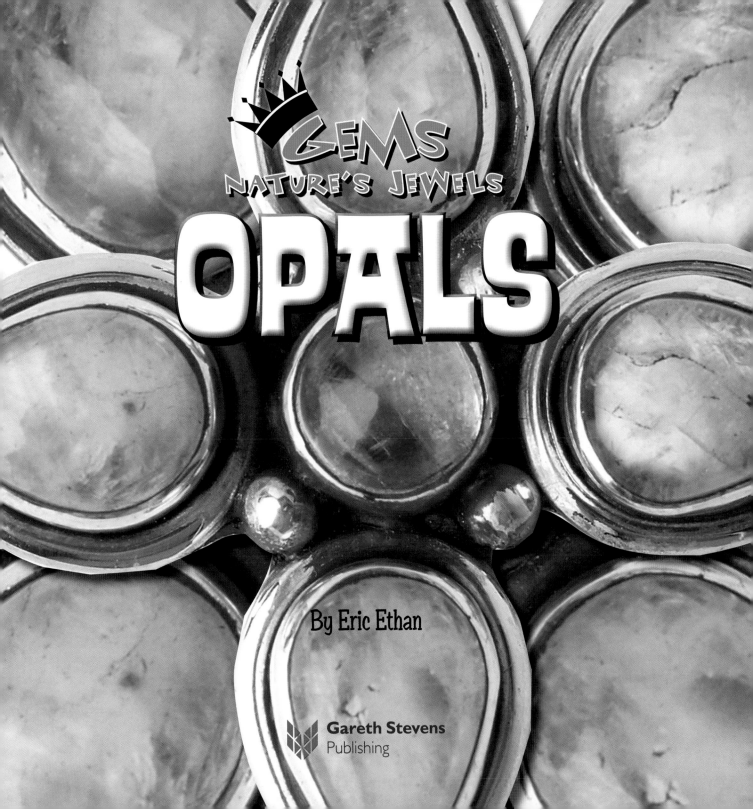

GEMS
NATURE'S JEWELS
OPALS

By Eric Ethan

Gareth Stevens
Publishing

Please visit our Web site, www.garethstevens.com. For a free color catalog of all our high-quality books, call toll free 1-800-542-2595 or fax 1-877-542-2596.

For Michelle, a real gem.

Library of Congress Cataloging-in-Publication Data

Ethan, Eric.
Opals / Eric Ethan.
    p. cm. — (Gems, nature's jewels)
Includes index.
ISBN 978-1-4339-4724-7 (pbk.)
ISBN 978-1-4339-4725-4 (6-pack)
ISBN 978-1-4339-4723-0 (lib. bdg.)
1. Opals—Juvenile literature. 2. Mineralogy—Juvenile literature. I. Title.
QE394.O7E84 2012
553.8'73—dc22

                              2010031735

First Edition

Published in 2012 by
Gareth Stevens Publishing
111 East 14th Street, Suite 349
New York, NY 10003

Copyright © 2012 Gareth Stevens Publishing

Designer: Haley W. Harasymiw
Editor: Greg Roza

Photo credits: Cover, p. 1 Hemera Technologies/PhotoObjects.net/Thinkstock; pp. 4, 5, 8, 9, 13, 15, 19, 21 Shutterstock.com; p. 7 De Agostini Picture Library/Getty Images; p. 11 Visuals Unlimited/Getty Images; p. 17 Peter Harholdt/SuperStock/Getty Images.

Printed in the United States of America

CPSIA compliance information: Batch #CS11GS: For further information contact Gareth Stevens, New York, New York at 1-800-542-2595.

CONTENTS

Words in the glossary appear in **bold** type the first time they are used in the text.

What Are Opals?

An opal looks as if a beautiful rainbow is caught inside the stone. Opals are formed from one of the most common elements on Earth—silica. Sand is also made of silica. However, gem-**quality** opal is **rare**.

Opals have a high water content compared to most other gems. They're sometimes called a **mineral** gel. This means they're soft. It's very easy to cut and shape raw opals into **polished** gemstones. However, they also break easily.

4

This collection of gem-quality opals shows all the colors of the rainbow. ▲

5

Where Are Opals Found?

Nearly all gem-quality opals come from southern Australia. The country has a few large opal mines, but most of the mines are small. Mines are often worked by just a few people hoping to find gem-quality opals.

Most gem-quality opals come from Coober Pedy in South Australia. The ground in the area is soft and easy to dig through. Miners often find opals very close to the surface. The town of Lightning Ridge in New South Wales is famous for its black opals.

GEM JOURNAL

It's very hot in southern Australia. Opal miners once made homes in the tunnels they dug because it's cooler underground.

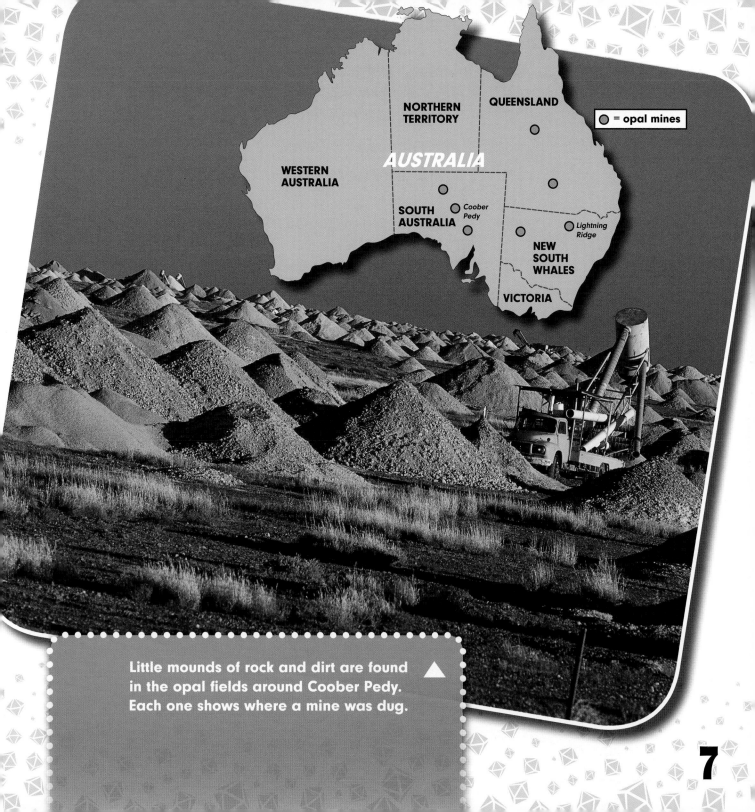

NORTHERN
TERRITORY

QUEENSLAND

= opal mines

WESTERN
AUSTRALIA

AUSTRALIA

SOUTH
AUSTRALIA

*Coober
Pedy*

*Lightning
Ridge*

NEW
SOUTH
WHALES

VICTORIA

Little mounds of rock and dirt are found
in the opal fields around Coober Pedy.
Each one shows where a mine was dug.

What Do Opals Look Like?

All opals **reflect** more than one color of light. The colors change as the stone is turned. It's the flashes of changing color that make opals so beautiful when worn as **jewelry**.

Gem-quality opals come in every color of the rainbow.

◄ This large uncut opal shows the mineral's natural color and beauty.

▼ The opal shown here is still in the rock in which it was found.

White and green opals are the most common and least **valuable**. Most opal mined in Australia is white and green. Black opals with red coloring are hard to find. Jewelry made from black opals is very valuable.

Mining Opal

Most opal miners dig a **shaft** until they find a shiny gray rock. They carefully remove small amounts of the rock. If miners are lucky, they soon see a rainbow-colored rock. This is an opal **deposit**. They remove this carefully and take it to be washed.

Large opal-mining businesses use bulldozers to remove a lot of dirt quickly. When they reach an opal deposit, they collect it with hand tools. This is more expensive than shaft mining, but it's quicker.

GEM JOURNAL

Opal **nuggets** were first discovered lying on the ground in South Australia. Finding opal is much harder now.

This gem-quality opal was found in a narrow deposit in a South Australian mine.

Finding a Gem

The stone from an opal mine is washed. Since there's very little water in the desert where the stones are found, miners load rock and some water into a cement truck drum. The drum spins and washes away the dirt.

Next, miners sort the remaining rock by hand. In its natural state, raw opal may not look like much. It takes a careful miner to find opal mixed in with lots of other rocks. Sometimes miners miss good pieces.

GEM JOURNAL

Miners called "noodlers" look for, and sometimes find, good opals in waste rock left behind at old claims.

Small opal-mining businesses use simple machines like this to move loose rock from the mine to the surface.

Making Opal Jewelry

Turning raw opal stone into jewelry requires careful work. Opal is only about as hard as window glass. It can break easily when a jeweler is working on it.

Nearly all opals are cut from other rocks using diamond-tipped saws and lots of water. The jeweler works carefully to remove only waste rock and keep as much of the opal as possible. The value of a finished opal depends a lot on its size.

GEM JOURNAL

Since most opals contain a lot of water, raw opals can actually dry out. When this happens, it makes the opal hard and easily cracked.

Black opals, like these beautifully finished stones, make the most expensive opal jewelry. ▲

Shaping and Polishing

A jeweler shapes and polishes the raw opal to bring out its bright colors. The back side of an opal gem is usually flat. A thin piece of darker, harder stone is attached to the back of the opal. This makes it easier to mount the gem in a setting. It also makes the opal's colors brighter and prettier. Most opal jewelry has a bezel setting. Gold or silver is wrapped around the lower edge of the opal to keep it safe.

GEM JOURNAL

Opals are too soft to be cut with flat surfaces. All opal gemstones come in a rounded cabochon (KA-buh-shahn) shape.

This old-fashioned necklace has very high-quality black opals set with rubies and diamonds.

17

What Makes Opals Valuable?

The larger and more colorful an opal is, the more valuable the jewelry made from it will be. Black opals from South Australia are the rarest and most valuable. Depending on the light, the color of a black opal can range from jet black to dark blue.

Black opal with red stripes is called red fire opal. It's the most expensive opal. Black opal with green or blue stripes is more common and less expensive.

GEM JOURNAL

In Australia, opal deposits are very thin. That means large opals are rare and more valuable.

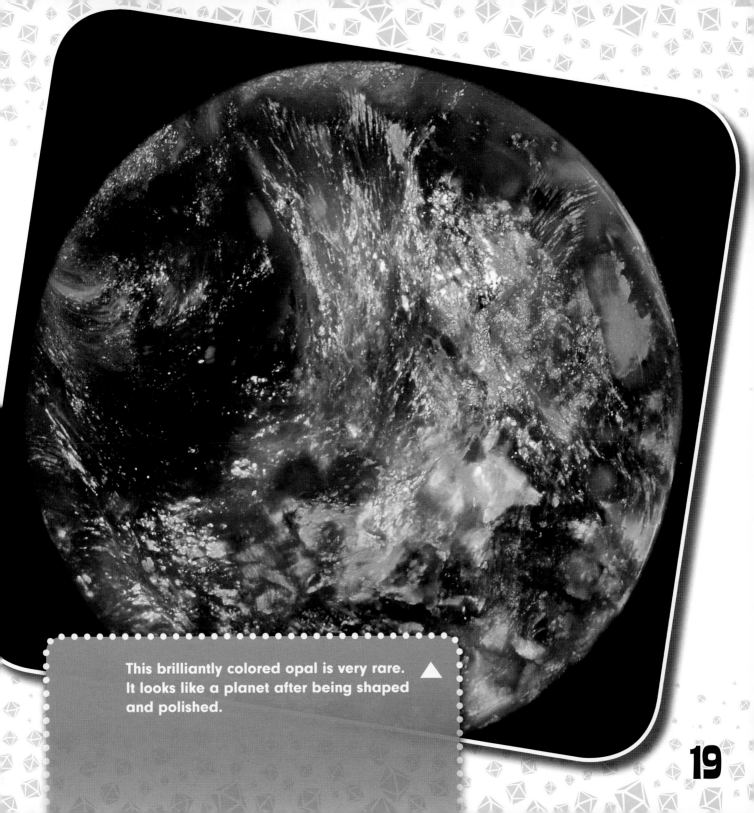

This brilliantly colored opal is very rare.
It looks like a planet after being shaped
and polished.

Really Rare Opals

The Aurora Australis black opal was found near Lightning Ridge in 1938. It's worth more than $850,000! It has bright splashes of red, blue, and green rarely seen in other opals.

The largest black opal ever found is called the Halley's Comet opal. It weighs about 14 ounces (400 grams)! It's as big as a man's hand and still hasn't been cut into individual gems. In 1986, the miners who discovered the Halley's Comet opal sold it for more than $1,000,000!

Know Your Opals

- Opal is the birthstone for the month of October.

- Opal was highly valued by the ancient Romans. Only emerald was considered more valuable.

- The native people of Australia called opal "Rainbow Serpent."

- The word "opal" may have come from the Sanskrit word "upala," which means "valuable stone."

- Opal is Australia's national stone.

- Australia produces more than 95 percent of the opal used in jewelry today.

- Man-made opal—first made in 1974— is called Gilson opal after its inventor, Pierre Gilson.

- Opal was recently discovered on Mars!

Glossary

deposit: an amount of a mineral in the ground that built up over a period of time

jewelry: pieces of metal, often holding gems, worn on the body

mineral: matter in the ground that forms rocks

nugget: a lump of valuable metal or a raw gemstone

polish: to make something smooth and shiny by rubbing it with a soft cloth

quality: the standard or grade of something

rare: uncommon or special

reflect: to give back light

shaft: a tunnel dug while mining

valuable: worth a lot of money

For More Information

Books

Petersen, Christine. *Groovy Gems*. Edina, MN: ABDO Publishing, 2010.

Symes, R. F., and R. R. Harding. *Crystal and Gem*. New York, NY: DK Publishing, 2007.

Web Sites

The Dynamic Earth
www.mnh.si.edu/earth/text
Explore gems, minerals, and mining at the National Museum of Natural History Web site.

The Mineral and Gemstone Kingdom
www.minerals.net
Read about gems and minerals.

Publisher's note to educators and parents: Our editors have carefully reviewed these Web sites to ensure that they are suitable for students. Many Web sites change frequently, however, and we cannot guarantee that a site's future contents will continue to meet our high standards of quality and educational value. Be advised that students should be closely supervised whenever they access the Internet.

Index